NUPTIALS

ISBN 0-8478-2269-9

LC 99 076991

First published in the United States of America in 2000 by
Rizzoli International Publications, Inc.
300 Park Avenue South
New York, NY 10010

Text and compilation copyright © Rebecca Buffum Taylor
Photography copyright © Joe Buissink
Package and concept copyright © Artful Giftworks. Artful Giftworks
is an imprint of Rizzoli International Publications, Inc.

Design by Hotfoot Studio

Distributed by St. Martin's Press

Printed and bound in China

NUPTIALS

Rebecca Buffum Taylor
Photography by Joe Buissink

Rizzoli
NEW YORK

Artful Giftworks

Be a lover as they are, that you come to know

your Beloved. Be faithful that you may know

Faith. The other parts of the universe did not accept

the next responsibility of love as you can.

—Rumi, "After Being in Love, the Next Responsibility"

PrEFaCe

WEDDINGS PULL DEEPLY ON THE COLLECTIVE IMAGINATION. THEY CELEBRATE THE
marriage of opposites—masculine and feminine, head and heart, impulse and reason—that are at
the core of nuptial rituals. This union brings a fire and heat that can burnish one's rougher
edges, as bride and groom experience the differences between man and woman, give and take,
and eros and agape. In large part, the magic of weddings is that they are an outward expres-
sion of this union of opposing forces.

Weddings are a bounty of choice. Each is a Rorshach of a couple's ideals and perceptions
of the themes of marriage: kisses, insatiability, trust, devotion, spirituality, and one's beloved.
Weddings are both highly personal and communal. They are intensely intimate as well as a
public display of affection.

Throughout history and around the world, weddings share a surprisingly common palette of
symbols, a universal language of love and commitment to something beyond oneself. Flowers
and flower children symbolize hope for a couple's fertility. A bride's appearance in virtually every
culture is attended to with great care, usually by other women, an allusion to the passing down
of feminine wisdom that prepares a woman to be married. A sacred circle is drawn—by fire, in
the sand, or simply in the mind—as part of many indigenous weddings, signifying the sacred space
within which a couple has chosen to honor each other. In rural India, a Hindu priest binds a
bride and groom together with bits of their clothing, literally tying a nuptial knot, before the
married couple walks bound together around a fire seven times, ritualizing their shared path
through life. Masks and mirrors call ancestral spirits to attend and witness nuptial rituals.

But perhaps the most touching and romantic of symbolic gestures is the wearing of a wedding veil. From Greek antiquity to the Victorian era, the wedding veil has guarded a bride from dangerous spirits who might approach her from other realms during that liminal phase when she moves across the delicate space between her past self as an individual and her new self within a couple. She wears the veil during her journey between two worlds, a veil that is lifted as she moves forward into a new realm. Her chosen groom often lifts the lace between their separate worlds and reveals her as a wholly new creature, so they can gaze upon each other's faces fully as they cross over together.

As with any major life transition, a wedding is an archetypal initiation with distinct phases. It begins with a deep calling—the engagement—the longing to create a lasting union with one's beloved. There follows a period of transition from being one-alone to one-in-relation to another. The wedding itself marks the stepping across the threshold to a joined life. Finally, a wedding reception marks the beginning of the couple's coming home, their return into their circle of families and friends as well as a reintegration into the larger circle of community.

Marrriage is an act of great courage coupled with trust. Perhaps no other edge is as sharp in its demands on an individual. While it is the wedding that opens the door to a new world, it is marriage that both tests and braces a couple, pushing them to the edge of their limits and far beyond. Perhaps it is this commitment to growth that brings the sense of expansion and possibility to weddings. Neither bride nor groom may know exactly where the marriage will take them, but they agree to journey there together.

Whatever a couple's individual ritual, weddings gently nudge into life the ancient archetype of the *hieros gamos*, the sacred marriage of god and goddess, the mythical marriage of goddess and king. Weddings are rituals that draw their witnesses closer together in the circle of humanity. They are a universal rite of passage that yearn to be deeply honored and lingered over with great care and attention.

Joe Buissink brings just this sense of exquisite care to his work as a wedding photographer. The attention he brings to the details and gestures of a wedding tell us something about the nature of commitment. While he follows classic aesthetic rules, the moments he captures are thoroughly unique, allowing him to discover that most illusive place where photojournalism and fine art meet.

Buissink's images are, like today's weddings themselves, a marriage of opposites: classical and original, elegant and natural, spontaneous and controlled. He creates indelible images not just of weddings, but of informal romance and savvy rebellion, with a visual sophistication far from the stiff, contrived tableaus that document most weddings. The result: timeless images of hope, surprise, and the enduring power of the human heart.

—Rebecca Buffum Taylor

i thank You God for most this amazing

day: for the leaping greenly spirits of trees

and a blue true dream of sky; and for everything

which is natural which is infinite which is yes

—E. E. Cummings (untitled)

To hear as a sandcrab hears the waves,

loud as a second heart;

to see as a green thing sees the sun,

with the undividing attention of blind love.

—Jane Hirshfield, "Rain in May"

Love is a high inducement to the individual to ripen,

to become something in himself, to become world,

to become world for himself for another's sake.

—Rainer Maria Rilke, *Letters to a Young Poet*

Love one another, but make not a bond of love:

let it rather be a moving sea between the shores of your souls.

—Kahlil Gibran, *The Prophet*

Within the body are gardens,

rare flowers, peacocks, the inner Music;

within the body a lake of bliss,

on it the white soul-swans take their joy.

—Mirabai, "O Friend, Understand"

Man and woman become one,

a physically and spiritually creative unity,

by virtue of their dissimilarity.

—Isak Dinesen, *On Modern Marriage and Other Observations*

MY LOVE WAS DEEP AND GENTLE AS THE SEAS

AND ROSE TO HER AS TO A CLIFF THE TIDE.

—Charles Baudelaire, "The Jewels"

The way the night knows itself with the moon,

be that with me. Be the rose

nearest the thorn that I am.

I want to feel myself in you when you taste food, in the arc

of your mallet when you work.

—Rumi, "In the Arc of Your Mallet"

WHEN WE FINALLY KISS

I SAY, "GIVE ME YOUR TALLEST.

LET IT BE A LONG WAY

DOWN FROM HERE."

—Tess Gallagher, "Do I Like It?"

All the wishes of my mind know your name,

And the white desires of my heart

They are acquainted with you.

The cry of my body for completeness,

That is a cry to you.

—Mary Carolyn Davies, "Love Song"

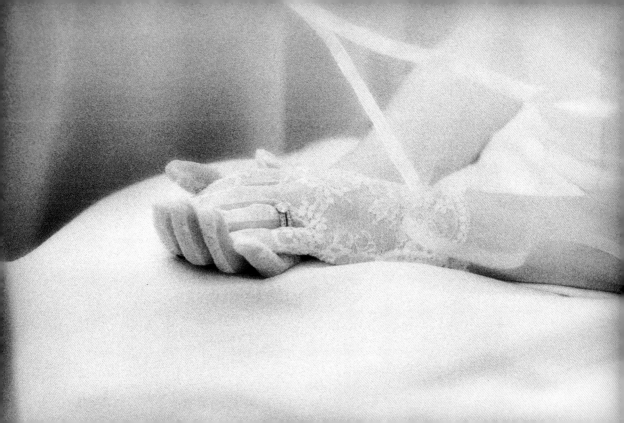

Love hath a language of his own

A voice that goes

From heart to heart—whose mystic tone

Love only knows.

—Persian poem

Let me not to the marriage of true minds

Admit impediments. Love is not love

Which alters when it alteration finds,

Or bends with the remover to remove.

O no! It is an ever-fixed mark

That looks on tempests and is never shaken.

—William Shakespeare, "Let Me Not to the Marriage of True Minds"

Learning to love differently is hard

love with the hands wide open, love

with the doors banging on their hinges,

the cupboard unlocked, the wind

roaring and whimpering in the rooms

rustling the sheets and snapping the blinds . . .

—Marge Piercy, "To Have without Holding"

From the moment of Time's

      first-drawn breath,

Love resides in us,

A treasure locked into the heart's

      hidden vault.

—Bibi Hayati, "Before There Was a Truce"

KEEP A GREEN TREE IN YOUR HEART

AND ONE DAY THE SINGING BIRD WILL COME.

—Chinese proverb

My heart cries out for you, my bride, my sister who has torn

my heart with her eyes like a bead from a necklace.

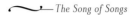—*The Song of Songs*

My heart wags me, a big dog

with a bigger tail. I am

a new coin printed with

your face.

—Marge Piercy, "Will We Work Together?"

For one human being to love another:

    that is perhaps the most difficult of all our tasks,

        the ultimate, the last test and proof,

            the work for which all other work is but preparation.

—Rainer Maria Rilke, *Letters to a Young Poet*

The minute I heard my first love story

I started looking for you, not knowing

how blind that was.

Lovers don't finally meet somewhere.

They're in each other all along.

—Rumi, "Music Master"

COME LIVE WITH ME AND BE MY LOVE,

AND WE SHALL ALL THE PLEASURES PROVE.

—Christopher Marlowe, "The Passionate Shepherd to His Love"

Then I will leap into Love—

And from Love into Knowledge,

And from Knowledge into the Harvest,

That sweetest Fruit beyond human sense.

There I will stay with You, whirling.

—Mechtild of Magdeburg, "Unless You Lead Me"

I wonder by my troth, what thou and I

Did, till we loved?

—John Donne, "The Good Morrow"

May it be beautiful before me,

May it be beautiful behind me,

May it be beautiful below me,

May it be beautiful above me,

May it be beautiful all around me,

May it be beautiful before me.

I am restored in beauty.

— Traditional Navajo prayer

Let them be lovers; let them behold truth; and their eyes are uplifted,

their wrinkles smoothed, they are perfumed again with hope and power.

—Ralph Waldo Emerson, *Emerson's Essays*

Heart, are you great enough

For a love that never tires?

O heart, are you great enough for love?

—Alfred, Lord Tennyson, "Marriage Morning"

'I saw you take his kiss!' 'Tis true.'

'O, modesty!' 'Twas strictly kept:

He thought me asleep; at least I knew

He thought I thought he thought I slept.'

—Coventry Patmore, "The Kiss"

An eye is meant to see things.

The soul is here for its own joy.

A head has one use: for loving a true love.

Legs: to run after.

—Rumi, "Someone Digging in the Ground"

O blush not so! O blush not so!

Or I shall think you knowing;

And if you smile the blushing while,

Then maidenheads are going.

—John Keats, "Sharing Eve's Apple"

Drink to me only with thine eyes,

And I will pledge with mine;

Or leave a kiss but in the cup,

And I'll not look for wine.

—Ben Jonson, "Song to Celia"

No beauty she doth miss

When all her robes are on:

But Beauty's self she is

When all her robes are gone.

—Seventeenth-century madrigal

At last they are able to meet

inside the white kiss where the spider's

tender silk has crosshatched their lips

with the musky taste of the never-before

as it enters the never-again.

—Tess Gallagher, "White Kiss"

here is the deepest secret nobody knows

(here is the root of the root and the bud of the bud

and the sky of the sky of a tree called life, which grows

higher than soul can hope or mind can hide)

and this is the wonder that's keeping the stars apart

i carry your heart (i carry it in my heart)

—E. E. Cummings (untitled)

Everything loves this way,

in gold honey,

in gold mountain grass

that carries lightly the shadow of hawks,

the shadow of clouds passing by.

—Jane Hirshfield, "For a Wedding on Mt. Tamalpais"

PERSONAL ACKNOWLEDGMENTS

To my father Justinus Theodorus Buissink.

Thanks to Rebecca, for her original vision for this project and her commitment and patience in making it fly.

I am grateful to all the couples who shared transcendent moments of their wedding days with me and
generously allowed me to print them in this book. I would especially like to thank my wife, Carrie, and my
children, Benjamin and Sarah, without whom none of this would be possible.

—Joe Buissink

The Wedding Box has been truly a labor of love. Many thanks to Marta Hallett, Elizabeth Sullivan, and
Signe Bergstrom at Rizzoli; and to Caroline Herter, PJ Bell, and Rebecca Kondos for your faith and support.
To Joe, of course, for your unique eye and big heart.
And to all lovers everywhere, who make their leaps of faith.

—Rebecca Taylor